The Cast of Monster Girls!

NISHIZURU YATSUKI

Works part-time in Akihabara. Can see ghosts, and got himself mixed up with a bunch of yokai.

NISHIZURU NANAO

Yatsuki's sister. She's been stuck as a spirit for the past six years, unable to return to her comatose body.

YOU'RE GETTING CARRIED AWAY...

KAPPER-VERT-SAN!!

AYATSUKI ROKKA

A pretty girl whom Yatsuki once helped out. She seems quite taken with him since then. She's actually a yokai: a rokurokubi.

SHIJOUIN DOLCE & GAPPANYA
A stuffed animal who freeloads at Yatsuki's grampa's place, and does nothing but pick fights with Rokka. Is actually a yokai: a hinnagami.

CHITOSEYA NAGI
A cosplay fortune-teller in Akihabara. Momo's older sister. An expert in the yokai situation in Akihabara. She sees real potential in Yatsuki, and has requested his help in managing yokai.

KAKINOKI MITSUO
Serves Nagi as her loyal retainer. Is actually a yokai: a kakiotoko.

CHITOSEYA MOMO
A maid who works at the maid cafe Yatsuki often goes to. By nature, is prone to being possessed by spirits and yokai. Her maid alias is "Moru."

SUZUNARI NIA
Sharp, athletic, and incredibly cool and beautiful, she's Rokka's classmate.

AIZAWA KEI
Momo's classmate at Kanda Izumi Girl's School and her childhood friend.

MAKABE ICHIE
Also known as Icchan. Rokka's friend, who's also ended up freeloading at Yatsuki's grampa's place. She's actually a yokai: a nurikabe.

The Story So Far

Nishizuru Yatsuki is a twenty-year-old virgin who works part-time at a general store in Akihabara. For some reason, he's also always been able to see spirits. Then one day, he meets the beautiful Rokka. She's super-cute, and happenstance brings them very close very fast... Or it would have, but Rokka turns out to be a yokai--a rokurokubi!

Since then, Yatsuki's life has been filled with yokai incidents! Moru, a maid at Yatsuki's favorite maid cafe, gets possessed by a kakiotoko. Then a slicing fiend, a hinnagami, attacks the girls on Flyer Road.

With all this going on, Yatsuki has started doing "yokai management" under Nagi's command. He's doing it to save his little sister, Nanao, who has been stuck as a spirit unable to return to her body. Meanwhile, Rokka has started attending Moru's school, and there, she senses a threatening presence near Moru...

TA—DAA!

CUTE, RIGHT? ♡

It's a hakama-style skirt!

LOOK, LOOK, JUNKER-SAN! A NEW UNIFORM, YEP! ♡

THUMP

ACK!

RUSTLE RUSTLE

PITTER PATTER PITTER

20
My Hero! ♪

ANYWAY, MORU-CHAN SERIOUSLY HASN'T SAID *ANYTHING* ABOUT ME?

YEAH, SURE IS CUTE. (monotone)

Ugh, that startled me!

WHY DO YOU KEEP ASKING?!

N-NO REA-SON.

You keep going on about that.

SHE HASN'T MENTIONED YOU! HOW MANY TIMES DO YOU NEED TO HEAR IT?

!

SO WHEN YOU SAY HAKAMA-STYLE, DOES THAT MEAN IT'S LIKE SHORTS?

WAIT ...

THAT REMINDS ME...

HM?

LIKE THAT GAME YOU PLAY WHEN YOU'RE KIDS.

THAT'S LIKE...

YOU KNOW...

LIKE "HIGH-HIGH ALPS" OR "PATTY CAKE" AND STUFF.

WHAT'S THAT *THING* YOU'RE ALWAYS DOING TOGETHER?

Where you clap hands.

OH, THAT?

I THINK IT WAS AROUND SECOND GRADE?

AND I COULDN'T DO IT AT ALL...

ON TOP OF MOUNT YARI...

THE ALPS ARE TEN THOU-SAND SHA-KU HIGH!...

*High High Alps, or Arupusu Ichiman Jaku (The Alps are Ten Thousand Shaku High), is a clapping game like Patty Cake, set to the tune of Yankee Doodle.

PAAANT...

WSH

HUH?

・・・・・・

I-IS SOME-
THING
WRONG?

・・・・・・

JUST MY
IMAGINA-
TION...I
GUESS?

PAAANT...

I WANT
TO
TOUCH
HER...

I WANT
TO
TOUCH
HER...!

PAAANT...

CLICK...

PAAANT...

GOOD
NIGHT,
THEN!

I
WANT
TO
TOUCH
HER!!

PAAANT...

PROTEC-
TION...

MORU-
CHAN, ARE
YOU O...

ALL
THOSE
OTHER
TIMES,
TOO!?

SAVE
ME?

DID
HE
JUST
...

HUH
...?

THERE'S
NO...
WAY...
RIGHT?

We're
not so
close
that
he'd go
out of
his way
just to
help me
out.

Sorry

CREAK...

HUH?

HUH
?!

WHY
ARE YOU
HERE?
WHAT'S
GOING
ON...?

CLANG

DOING THIS KIND OF THING WITH ANOTHER GIRL....

IS WEIRD...

YEAH...

・・・・・・

I MEAN...

I AM WEIRD...

SINCE WE FIRST MET...

STOP... THIS...

Ah...

SHIVER

SHIVER

Hnn...

THIS ISN'T RIGHT...

WHAT THE HELL...

ARE YOU TWO?

It... cut my cheek...

ZU

ZU

ZU

IF YOU'RE GONNA INTERRUPT MY FUN TIME...

ZU

I'LL KILL YOU!!!!

ZU

IS THIS THE TIME TO BE IMPRESSED?!

MY RAZOR IS BROKEN.

With her bare hands... Whoa!

HUH...?

HM?

ROKKA-CHAN?!

THIS ROKU-ROKUBI ATTACKED... AND THEN...

YOU'VE GOT IT WRONG!

Y...

·············

SQUEAK...

!

SH-SHE'S JUST PASSED OUT, RIGHT?!

UH, YEAH.

BOOBS!!

HIGH

Erm! Eep!

BA-BA-BWOIING

おぱぽじ

ん

ZU ZU ZU

YOU SON OF A BITCH...

ZU ZU ZU

YOU STINK!

YOU'RE A SPIRITU- ALIST?!

ZU

ZU

NO ONE'S EVER CALLED ME *THAT* BEFORE!

It sounds kinda funky!

OH!

"Spiritualist"!

HI GH

. . . . .

NOW SOME- ONE *ELSE* IS INTER- RUPTING US.

FWUMP...

SORRY, MOMO...

Relevant to My Interests

ZU

AIZAWA KEI, HUH... I SEE.

And Rokka?

RIGHT NOW, SHE'S MAKING A HANDY ARMREST FOR ME.

THE HUMAN JUST CAME IN, AND THEY'RE FIGHTING.

OR MORE LIKE, HE'S JUST BEING A SAND-BAG.

GON!!

DOSU DOSU ドス ドス

AIZAWA KEI WILL *BREAK*.

I'M HEADING YOUR WAY IN A TAXI, BUT IT'LL TAKE ANOTHER FIFTEEN MINUTES.

ガガ VRRRM

LISTEN... *ALL OF YOU* NEED TO STOP AIZAWA KEI, AS FAST AS YOU CAN.

IF YOU DON'T...

Normally, humans can only use about thirty percent of the strength in their bodies.

WHAT DO YOU MEAN?

HE DOESN'T *NEED* TO BEAT HER...!!

MUSCLE FIBERS AND TENDONS WOULD SNAP, CAPILLARIES BURST, BONES BREAK.

THAT'S BECAUSE IF YOU WERE ALWAYS OUTPUTTING A HUNDRED PERCENT...

THEN YOUR BODY COULDN'T WITHSTAND THE BURDEN.

YOU'RE THEIR **PUPPET**, SO TO SPEAK. SO THE BODY'S SELF-PRESERVATION MECHANISMS WON'T KICK IN. OF COURSE, YOU'LL ALSO FEEL NO PAIN.

YOU'LL CONTINUE FIGHTING WITH ONE HUNDRED PERCENT OF YOUR STRENGTH UNTIL YOUR BODY BREAKS DOWN AND YOU CAN'T MOVE ANY LONGER.

BUT IF YOU'RE **POSSESSED**, THINGS ARE DIFFERENT.

THE HUMAN CAN'T BEAT HER, Y'KNOW?

WHAT DO WE **DO** EXACTLY, THOUGH?

SO *THAT'S* HOW SHE BROKE MY RAZOR SO EASILY!

I GET IT.

....

There's no way I can lose!

THAT'S IT! I JUST NEED TO FIND MY CHANCE SOME~ WHERE...

SHE SURE DOESN'T HIT LIKE A GIRL!

JUST WHAT THE HELL IS SHE?!

TREMBLE

AH...

GAH!

TREMBLE

TREMBLE

THAT'S RIGHT! I CAN'T LOSE THIS!

Chance! Chance~!

Wow, wow, wow!

DA-DALAAA! DA-DALA-DA-DAA! DAA-LAA-LAA! DALA-DALA~!

WAIT...

DA-DALAAA! DA-DALA-DA-DAA! DAA-LAA-LADALA! DA-DAAA~!

You've gotta grab hold of it! Hey~!!

Chance! Chance~!

Wow, wow, wow!

※ Shijouin is singing "Diamond Happy," the second opening song for the anime adaptation of Aikatsu!, an arcade collectible card game about idol singers.

WHY THE HELL ARE YOU SING-ING?! HEY!!

Look up, the sun is sparkling! Shine brighter, even brighter~!

You shiiine, diamond~!

TRUST
ME...!!

LET'S BEGIN!

24
First Love... ♪

IT MAY HURT A BIT, BUT BEAR WITH IT.

I'LL BE EXORCISING WHAT'S POSSESSING YOU.

NAGI-SAN, I...

NO...

THAT'S NOT WHAT I...

IT'S OKAY! ONEECHAN DOES THIS A LOT. DON'T WORRY!

MOMO, I REALLY DO...

MOMO...

BEFORE WE BEGIN, I'LL ASK YOU TWO OR THREE QUESTIONS.

I REALLY DO...

HAVE YOU RECENTLY... GONE TO A RIVER, POND OR LAKE?

LICENTIOUS... WHAT?

AND DID YOU ENGAGE IN ANY LICENTIOUS CONDUCT THERE?

WE WENT SWIMMING IN THE RIVER OUT BACK...

DURING THE LONG WEEKEND LAST MONTH, I WENT WITH SOME GIRLS ON THE TEAM TO MY GRAMPA'S HOUSE IN THE COUNTRY.

OH...

OH!

BUT...

NO! I HAVEN'T DONE THAT!!

Definitely not!

AH!

We'll get bug bites...

No... We can't do it here...

AH!

AH!

SEXUAL INTERCOURSE OR ANYTHING CLOSE.

AHN!

Out-doors?!

Kei-chan?!

SHE HAS?!

THIS PALM BE NOT MINE OWN, BUT A HEAVENLY SPIRIT RESIDING IN ETERNITY...

URK...

ZU ZU

IF THE HAND BE DEIFIED, AND WE DIVINE...

ALL MANNER OF SPIRIT SHALL BE CLEANSED...

ALL MANNER OF SPIRIT SHALL BE CLEANSED...

YOU CAN DO IT!

KEI-CHAN...

THE HAND OF SUKUNA HIKONA... IF THE HAND BE DEIFIED, AND WE DIVINE...

ZU

THAT WHICH POS-SESSES AIZAWA KEI...

OH... YEAH!

HAS SHE EVER SAID THE PHRASE, "KICKED BY A KAPPA"?

AGH...

THIS PALM BE NOT MINE OWN, BUT A HEAVENLY SPIRIT RESIDING IN ETERNITY...

THE HAND OF SUKUNA HIKONA...

ZU ZU

SHE SAID EXACTLY THAT.

Relevant

BOY.

Relevant to M

ZU

IS MOST CERTAIN-LY...

THE POSSESSION CONSUMES HER, BODY AND SPIRIT, AND ULTIMATELY, SHE WILL BECOME SEVERELY ILL AND DIE.

WHEN POSSESSED BY A KAPPA, A NORMALLY TIMID WOMAN WILL SAY LEWD THINGS AND BECOME SO SALACIOUS AS TO WOO ANYONE AND EVERYONE...

LEGENDS SAY THAT IF A WOMAN ACTS IN A LICENTIOUS MANNER NEAR A BODY OF WATER, A KAPPA WILL BECOME INFATUATED WITH HER.

POSSESSION BY A KAPPA...

GENERALLY, A MALE KAPPA WILL POSSESS A HUMAN WOMAN AND CAUSE LEWD BEHAVIOR WITH HUMAN MEN...

BUT IN THIS CASE, FOR SOME REASON, KEI ONLY APPROACHED MOMO, ANOTHER WOMAN, WITH THAT SORT OF BEHAVIOR...

YOU'RE...

A LESBIAN, AREN'T YOU?

MOMO...?

LISTEN...

MY FIRST LOVE...

I WAS REALLY IN LOVE...

BUT IT DIDN'T GO ANYWHERE.

WAS ENERGETIC, CHEERFUL, AND REALLY ATHLETIC...

POPULAR WITH BOTH BOYS AND GIRLS...

AND A LITTLE DUMB, BUT HATED TWISTED PEOPLE, AND WAS A REALLY STRONG AND KIND PERSON.

NO! I DIDN'T SAY ANYTHING.

?

DID YOU CONFESS TO THEM?

BE-CAUSE...

Extra Manga ~Kappa Possession, as Seen from Moru's POV~

Extra Manga ~So How Far Did We Go?~

SO HUMID...

MIIN.

MIN MIN

MIN ——...

SO HOTT ...

MIIN

MIN MIN

SIMMER

SIMMER

MIIN —...!!

SIMMER

25
Something I Want to Make Sure of

HYUU

HAH!

I'M IMPRESSED HE'S STILL AT IT NOW.

IT REALLY IS *SO DAMN HOT.*

Ahh...

Haah...!

DON'T KNOW ...

Haah... Haah...

IT'S SO DAMN HOT, EVERY DAY... AGH...

WHERE'D THE RAINY SEASON GO?

HYUU

HAH!

※ In the story, it's early July. ♪

Ohhh!

Huh?! There's another one?!

HIS GRANDPA CAME OUT WITH AN EXTRA, FOR SAFE-KEEPING.

Here.

ONE FOR SAFE-KEEP-ING?!

THEN DOES THAT MEAN HE HAS ONE MORE FOR LENDING, TOO*?!

OH, WHEN HE WENT TO HIS GRANDPA TO APO-LOGIZE...

HYUUF

Hah!

AND WHERE DID THAT WOODEN SWORD COME FROM? I THOUGHT THE JOROUGUMO SLICED IT UP.

HYUU   Hah!

SPRAWL

HYUU   Hah!

SPRAWL

*There's a saying about serious otaku: they buy three copies of stuff they really love; one for use, one for safekeeping, and one to lend out.

HE ALSO STILL NEEDS TRAINING ON HOW TO GATHER ETHEREAL ENERGY.

SO RIGHT NOW, HE'LL STILL BE RELYING ON TOOLS LIKE THAT.

...IS COLLECTING AROUND HIS FISTS!!

THOUGH JUNKER-SAN CAN DO THOSE... ETHEREAL ATTACK THINGS NOW...

NAGI-SAN SAID THEY'RE NOT THAT STRONG.

TAKE

THIS TAKES ME BACK! I HAVEN'T SEEN HIM PRACTICING LIKE THIS FOR SO LONG!

HYUU

HYUU

IT TAKES YOU BACK?

POP

OH! YOU'RE DOING PRACTICE SWINGS!

WORD.

NICE, DEAD SLANG.

DON'T CALL IT "DEAD"!

WHEN HE'S FIGHTING A CUTE GIRL, HE SHRIVELS UP LIKE A PRUNE.

I DOUBT THE PROBLEM LIES WITH HIS WEAPONS. 'TIS HIS MENTAL WEAKNESS.

HELLO...

--TOR.

HUH? YOU DID?!

WELL, I DID TELL ROKKA-CHAN, BUT...

OH... IT'S OKAY! IT'S MY FAULT FOR BARGING IN UNANNOUNCED!

S-SORRY! I'M NOT DRESSED!!

ERP! SHIRT-LESS!!

M...M-M-M-MORU-CHAN?!

I'M SCARING MYSELF, NOW.

THAT'S A PRETTY PRECISE RESPONSE FOR SOMEONE HALF-ASLEEP.

YOU WERE ASLEEP THEN, WEREN'T YOU?

Dummy!

You were asleep?

Still.

Momo-chan

I know this is sudden, but... Could I maybe go to your place today, Rokka-chan?

Σd(>∀・)

Yay!
Okay, then I'll come by this afternoon then. ♡

ACK. ACK!

THE BONE GOT MESSED UP. AND SOME LIGAMENTS AND TENDONS HERE AND THERE!

IT'S NOT A BIG DEAL, THOUGH.

A-AIZAWA-SAN! YOUR...

!

I WAS THE ONE DOING THE BEATING, YET I'M THE ONE WHO'S BUSTED UP.

LAME, RIGHT?

MEANWHILE, YOU'RE AS HEALTHY AS A HORSE!

Hm?

OH, THIS?

I COULDN'T STOP YOU BEFORE THAT HAPPENED.

I'M SORRY...

BUT...

I'M THE ONE WHO SHOULD BE APOLOGIZING HERE!

WHY ARE *YOU* SAYING SORRY?

NO, I REALLY AM SORRY.

I DON'T REMEMBER EVERYTHING THAT HAPPENED, BUT...I THINK I WENT FULL-ON CRAZY.

SERIOUSLY... I'M SO SORRY!

H-HEY! IT'S NOT LIKE *YOU* DIDN'T WANT TO COME, MOMO!

SHE INSISTED ON COMING HERE TO APOLOGIZE IN PERSON!

OH! NO, UM...

I, UH, WELL...

HUH? YOU WANTED TO COME TOO, MORU-CHAN?!

OH!

HUH?

WHAT COULD THAT BE?

THERE IS SOME-THING...

I WANTED TO MAKE SURE OF.

MORU-CHA--

......

HEY, YOU *TALKED*, RIGHT?! YOU JUST SAID SOME-THING! YOU WERE EVEN MOVING AROUND!!

VA-VA--

VOOM!

I'M SURE OF IT NOW.

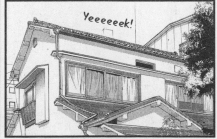

Yeeeeeek!

THE REASON MORU-CHAN CAME HERE IS TO GET SOLID PROOF...

AND DETERMINE WHETHER ROKKA AND THE HINNAGAMI REALLY ARE YOKAI...!!

WHAT ABOUT NANAO?

YOU TOO, NANAO!

GOT THAT?

YOU'D HAVE TO QUIT GOING TO SCHOOL, ROKKA!

IT'D BE A DISASTER IF SHE FOUND OUT! JUST KEEP THINGS LOW-KEY TODAY!

SEEING THAT STUFF ONCE, AND UNDER STRESSFUL CONDITIONS, ISN'T QUITE ENOUGH TO MAKE YOU BELIEVE.

AND I DON'T THINK SHE SAW THE KAPPA DURING THE POSSESSION, EITHER.

AND SHE ESPIED THE KAPPA'S POSSESSION, TOO.

WHAT OTHER PROOF DOES SHE NEED? ROKKA STRETCHED HER NECK RIGHT BEFORE HER EYES, DID SHE NOT?

I'VE GOT A BAD FEELING ABOUT THIS...

GOT IT!!

YEP!

SQUEEE! ♡

Holy cow!

SO MANY DIFFERENT KINDS!

They all look so good! ♡

BA-BAAAAM

DOES IT MATTER?

'TIS THE *MOST* IMPORTANT MATTER!

BUT WHAT'RE WE GOING TO DO ABOUT THE CAKES, JUNKER-SAN? WHO'S EATING WHICH?

DIBS ON THE STRAW-BERRY SHORT-CAKE! YEP!

HMPH! NEVER!!

CONK

Guh!

WHY YOU ...!!

I'M SORRY. I DIDN'T KNOW HOW MANY PEOPLE THERE WOULD BE, SO I JUST BROUGHT WHATEVER.

OH NO, THIS IS PLENTY! SORRY FOR MAKING YOU GO TO THE TROUBLE.

NO! WHAT MUST BE DONE...

WE SHOULD DO ROCK-PAPER-SCISSORS!

IS THAT!

GAH!

ST-STOP FIGHTING, YOU GUYS!

HUH? "CONK"?

STREEETCH

TUG TUG TUG

TWITCHING

REALLY WANT THE STRAW- BERRY SHORT- CAKE. ♡

I...

CUT THAT... OKAY! FINE, I GET IT!

I *REALLY* WANT... STRAW- BERRY SHORT- CAKE. ♡

HEY! WHAT'RE YOU SHOWING ME YOUR CLEAVAGE FOR?!

Oh!

ROKKA'S REALLY GOING FOR IT, HUH?

Wow...

WELL, I WAS FINE WITH ANYTHING, REALLY.

JUST THE SAD NATURE OF MEN, HUH?

HUBBA-HUBBA~...! ♡

TUG

So, like...

Soooo gooood! ♡

UH...

Y-YEAH!

ROKKA'S YOUR COUSIN, RIGHT, YAKKII-SAN?

OH, SO ANY- WAY!

MUNCH MUNCH

NOM NOM

EVEN IF YOU'RE COUSINS...

WE'VE COME BEARING TOKENS FOR YOUR HARD WORK.

GREAT. MORE PEOPLE TO BE ANXIOUS ABOUT.

OH! NAGI-SAN, YOU'RE NOT DRESSED UP!

That's unusual, yep!

I DO WEAR NORMAL CLOTHES, YOU KNOW.

WATER-MELON!

WE'VE BROUGHT FIRE-WORKS, TOO.

ONEE-CHAN!

I TOLD HER, "OBVIOUSLY NOT, BUT GO MAKE SURE OF THAT YOURSELF."

HEY... ONEE-CHAN!

URK!

OH, MOMO THINKS ROKKA MIGHT BE A YOKAI.

OH! I FOR-GOT!

You dummy.

SO? MOMO! HAVE YOU SEEN WHAT YOU CAME FOR?

WHAT'S THIS ABOUT?

MOMO...?

......

MORU-CHAN...

UM...

HUH?

OH...
UM...

Err...

WHY...

DID YOU GO THAT FAR TO PROTECT ME?

PEW PEW PEW

Oho ho ho ho!

Just you try to hit me!

Ack! That's dangerous! Stop!

WIGGLE

WIGGLE

GOOO!

YEAH! THAT'S RIGHT! YOUR SISTER ASKED ME!

SHE TOLD ME TO PROTECT YOU FOR HER!

SHE DID?

N-NAGI-SAN ASKED ME TO!

I'M NOT SURE IF I SHOULD REALLY BE ASKING THIS OR NOT, BUT...

CAN I...

ASK YOU ONE MORE THING?

Um...

YAKKII-SAN... LIKES...

OH... I SEE...

DON DON DON

No... body shots...

Ge geh!

YEAH! THAT'S IT! AHA HA HA HA!

THAT CAME OUT OF NO- WHERE!

WHAT?

NOT A BAD DODGE, IF I DO SAY SO MYSELF!

YAKKII-SAN...

WHAT KIND OF YOKAI ARE YOU?!

HUH?

YOU'RE ROKKA-CHAN'S COUSIN, SO THAT MUST MEAN YOU'RE A ROKU-ROKUBI TOO, RIGHT?

OH! BUT YOU'RE A MAN, SO DOES THAT MAKE YOU A MIKOSHI-NYUUDOU, THEN?

HUH...?

UM...

NO...

YOU CAN SURE TAKE A LOT OF HITS, SO YOU MUST BE A PRETTY STRONG YOKAI, RIGHT?

LIKE AN USHI-ONI?! OR DOES TAKE A LOT OF HITS MEAN YOU'RE A FUURI OR SOMETHING?!

SPACE BOY

※ A mikoshi-nyuudou is typically bald yokai, with an ever-extending neck. Said to frighten people who look over the top of things such as folding screens. An ushi-oni is an ox demon with a horned, bovine head; A fuuri is a monkey-like yokai that cannot be cut by blades or burnt by flames.

WOOH!!!

SPARKLE SPARKLE SPARKLE GLEEE!!

YOU CAN'T BE AN ONI OR A TENGU OR SOMETHING, RIGHT?!

UH...

※ An oni is an ogre-like yokai. A tengu is a winged yokai, usually depicted with red skin and a long nose.

Extra Manga ~Moru's Wild Fantasies ②~

WHAT KIND OF YOKAI ARE YOU, KAKINOKI-SAN?

YOU DON'T REMEMBER...?

KAPPA-SAN IS A HIN-NAGAMI... AND THEN NANAO-CHAN IS A GHOST?

That's right!♪

Yep!♥

ROKKA-CHAN'S A ROKURO-KUBI, AND ICCHAN'S A NURIKABE!

DO YAKKII-SAN AND KAKINOKI-SAN NOT GET ALONG?

SMACK

THEN I SHALL--

TUG

NOT SHOW HER!

NGH...

WHY DID YOU SAVE ME?

OR... MAYBE THEY JUST MAKE IT LOOK THAT WAY, WHEN ACTUALLY...

WE TOLD MORU-CHAN AND KEI-CHAN EVERYTHING.

THAT ROKKA, ICCHAN, THE HINNAGAMI, AND THE KAKIOTOKO ARE YOKAI.

YANK
POW
RE-STRAIN YOUR-SELF!
WRIGGLE=WRIGGLE
You too, Icchan?
M—hmm.

AND ALSO...

AND THAT I'M FIGHTING YOKAI...

TO RETURN MY SISTER, NANAO, TO HER BODY.

NOW THAT WE'D TOLD HER EVERYTHING, WE HAD HER PROMISE TO KEEP IT ALL A STRICT SECRET.

THAT MORU HERSELF IS NATURALLY PRONE TO BEING TARGETED BY YOKAI AND STUFF.

MEAN-WHILE, ROKKA WILL KEEP GOING TO SCHOOL AS SHE HAS BEEN.

ALL WAS WELL THAT ENDED WELL...

BUT...

FLUTTER ♡

REACHING THIS POINT...

RAISES NEW QUESTIONS ...

SO!

YAKKII-SAN...!

OH, COME ON! YOU'RE ROKKA'S COUSIN, SO THERE'S NO WAY YOU COULD BE HUMAN!

NO, LISTEN, I'M *HUMAN.*

IT'S OKAY! I'VE GOT TIGHT LIPS!

SPARKLE

SPARKLE

OMG! OMG!

SPARKLE

WHAT KIND OF YOKAI ARE *YOU?!*

SHE SEEMS SO HAPPY ...

BUT SHE'S TOTALLY GOT THE WRONG IDEA.

I'M GLAD THAT SHE'S TALKING TO ME LIKE SHE USED TO...

AGH...

．．．．．．

WHAT'RE WE GONNA DO NOW?

SO...

WE WEREN'T MAKING THEM LAUGH. WE WERE SCARING THEM!

HEH HEH ...

YEAH.

ALL WE HAD TO DO WAS **SCARE** PEOPLE.

THINGS USED TO BE SO GOOD.

THAT'S IT!

RISE

!

．．．．．．

28
Heaven's
Lost
Property ♡

UGH
...

YEEP!!

MONDAYS ARE SUCH A DRAG.

AND IT'S HOT, TOO.

THE BEGINNING OF ANOTHER WEEK.

HA HA...

!

BWA HA HA HA HA! IS THIS FOR REAL?! THAT'S SOME PRETTY HALF-ASSED COSPLAY!

YA GOTTA SHOW YOUR BALLS!

LOOK AT THIS! IT SAYS *HENTAI KAMEN* IS IN AKIBA!

WHOA-AA!! THERE HE IS!!!

LEAP 7

WAAUUUGH!!!

Eeeeek!
Yaaaah!

There he is again!

It's Hentai Kamen!

Ahh!!

Pervert!

Eeeeek!

HENTAI KAMEN...

HUH?

"AS OF NOW, EIGHT IDENTICAL INCIDENTS HAVE OCCURRED, AND THE NUMBER OF ARRESTS HAS CLIMBED TO SIX"...!

Underwear-Clad Menaces in Akihabara

Men are appearing frequently around Akihabara, wearing women's undergarments on their heads. Suspects testify that they fall unconscious, and upon awakening, find themselves wearing underwear on their heads. As of now, eight identical incidents have occurred, and the number of other private citizens

"SUSPECTS TESTIFY THAT THEY FALL UNCONSCIOUS, AND UPON AWAKENING, FIND THEM-SELVES WEARING UNDERWEAR ON THEIR HEADS.

"MEN ARE APPEARING FREQUENTLY AROUND AKIHABARA WEARING WOMEN'S UNDER-GARMENTS ON THEIR HEADS.

IF IT WERE ONLY EASIER TO FIND THIS STUFF, IT WOULDN'T BE SUCH A PAIN TO--

WELL, ANYWAY...

"GO, BOY! CAPTURE HENTAI KAMEN!!"

"THERE'S A POSSIBILITY THAT THEY'RE BEING CON-TROLLED BY SOME SORT OF YOKAI...

Hentai!! Hentai!! Hentai!!

!

EEEEK!!

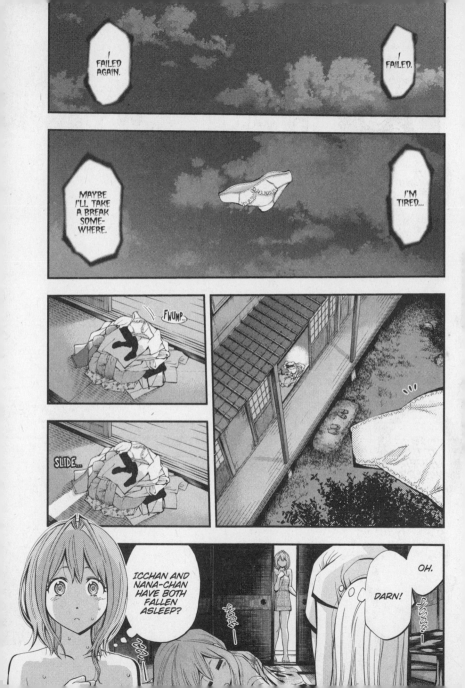

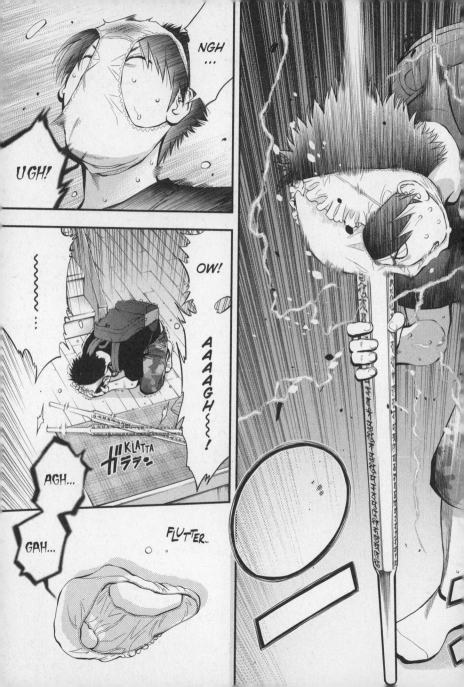

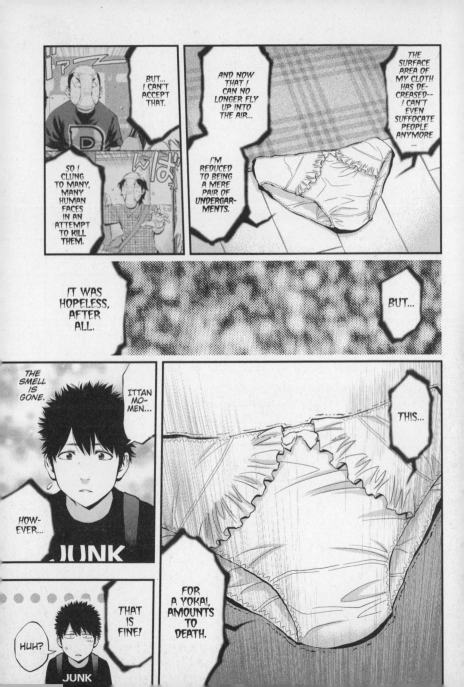

HAVING BEEN WORN AS A PAIR OF UNDER-GARMENTS JUST NOW...

I'VE REALIZED HOW WONDER-FUL IT IS!

FROM NOW ON, I WILL LIVE AS PANTIES! AND MY GOAL SHALL BE...

TO BE WORN BY A THOU-SAND WOMEN !!

FLOAT...

I'VE COME TO VISIT THE CAPE YOU ONCE TOLD ME OF. WE PROMISED WE WOULD GO TOGETHER, BUT NOW, THAT CANNOT BE SO.

THE BUS TO THE CAPE RUNS ALONG, AND THE BLUE SEA REACHES INTO THE SKY. ONCE I PLUNGE THIS SADNESS DEEP IN MY HEART, I WILL END THIS JOURNEY, AND RETURN TO TOWN.

WISH I GOT TO SEE MORU-CHAN SPORTING A PAIR LIKE THAT...

GLOOOON...

My dignity as the heroine...

SOB SOB

SOB

Monster Girls

Thank you very much for picking up Yokai Girls volume 3!

Yokai Girls started serialization in 2014, and it's all gone by in a flash! It's already 2015 now.. It had been a year since I'd last done a weekly serialization, so I wasn't quite able to get into the swing of things again. I really freaked out over a lot of things. But this year, I hope I can return to my previous pace so I can get things done besides drawing, like my hobbies and other stuff. Because frankly, I just stay cooped up at home every day drawing manga, so there's nothing for me to draw here (laughs)! Oh! Since I have the opportunity, I guess I'll draw my daily schedule here then? If you're not interested in that, then sorry!

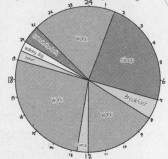

It's basically like this!
And then when you look at the week...

Mon	Tue	Wed	Thu	Fri	Sat	Sun
Sketches	Sketches	Inking	Inking	manga meeting	day off	Storyboards

Well, you get the idea..

Good! I've filled up all the space! (laughs)
And so, as I did last time, a cosplay illustration! →
This time it's Nanao doing AGRS's *Getsuei Gakuen*!
Thank you so much to Sugita Tomokazu-san for cheerfully giving me permission for this! I had fun drawing it!!

Now then, I hope you enjoy the rest of this volume! See you again in volume four! ♪

2014.12.3. Kazuki Funatsu

Official website: http://funatsukazuki.com/
Twitter: @funatsukazuki

Nanao @ AGRS

$$\int_1^4 \{(2x-2)-(2x^2-8x+6 \text{ SKRCH }\} dx$$

$$\int_1^4 (-2x^2+10x-8) dx$$

MISS SUZUNARI!

TLP...

OHHHH!
CLAP CLAP CLAP
CLAP CLAP

MAGNIFIQUE!

GREAT! I KNEW YOU'D DO WONDER-FULLY...

29

Girl With
the Peephole
Panties ♪

YOU GUYS WERE CRAZY FAST!

THAT WAS AMAZING! BOTH OF YOU WERE AMAZING!

ぱぁぁぁっ BEAAAM

BUT WOW, SUZU-NARI-SAN IS HARD-CORE, HUH?

AND SHE'S CUTE AND STYLISH, TOO.

IT'S LIKE THAT SAYING ABOUT HEAVEN NOT GIVING YOU MORE THAN ONE TALENT IS BULL, AM I RIGHT? YEP?!

SO...

I KNOW, RIGHT?!

SHE'S SMART AND ATHLETIC, TOO... BRAINS AND BRAWN!

AIZAWA! SUZUNARI! YOU HAVE TO JOIN OUR TRACK TEAM!!

JONES-SENSEI WAS DESPERATE TO RECRUIT YOU GUYS!

Let's aim for the inter-high to-gether!

YEP YEP, HE WAS EVEN CRYING, HUH?

HUH?

WHERE'D THOSE TWO GO, ANYWAY?

SHIVER

JOLT

OH! THERE SHE IS!

WHAT THE HELL?

SEE YOU.

I DON'T WANT TO DRAW TOO MUCH ATTENTION TO MYSELF.

SORRY.

IT'S JUST...

TAP...

I'VE FOUND YOU...!

Yokai Girls **3** End

HUH?! WHAT ARE YOU DOING?! WE DIDN'T AGREE TO THIS!

What are "followers"?

IN THIS SEGMENT, I'LL BE REPLYING TO QUESTIONS FROM MY FOLLOWERS!

TA-TA-TA-DAA!

SPECIAL PLAN!!

BY THE WAY, IF YOU WANT TO SAY "DO YOUR BEST," IT WOULD BE, "PANYANYAN DA!"

I JUST SORTA USE IT HOWEVER I WANT, THOUGH.

Like panyanaru! Or panyare! ♪ Or whatever.

UM, WELL! "PANYANYAN" MEANS "TO DO YOUR BEST" IN LAO! ♪

ພະຍາຍາມ

"WHAT DOES PANYANYAN MEAN?" YEP!

UM, FIRST UP IS A QUESTION FROM ACCOUNT NAME YAMAZAKI KENTAROU-SAN!

MY BIRTH OCCURRED UPON DECEMBER 18TH!

What point is there in asking that?

DUNNO!

MINE'S NOVEMBER 20TH! ♪

140cm

35cm

115cm

APRIL 8TH.

167cm

I WAS BORN AUGUST 10TH, YEP!

152cm

AND FROM FAKEME@ TREKKIE-HIKING-SAN: "I WANT TO KNOW WHAT ALL YOUR HEIGHTS ARE! PLEASE TELL ME!"

I GUESS I'LL JUST TELL YOU ALL OF 'EM AT ONCE!

NEXT! FROM IKARIYAMA YASUSADA-SAN: "PLEASE TELL US EVERYONE'S BIRTHDAYS."

WHAT DO I...? WELL...

STAAARE...

I GUESS...

HONESTLY SPEAKING, HOW DO YOU FEEL ABOUT ROKKA-CHAN?!

HUH? ME?!

NEXT! MOMOKA@LESSTWITTER*3DSCONFISCATED-SAN!

"QUESTION FOR JUNKER-SAN!"

I KINDA FEEL LIKE I JUST CAN'T IGNORE HER... BEING WITH HER IS FUN, AND SHE'S NEVER BORING, AND SHE'S GOT BIG BOOBS...

HONESTLY, SHE'S CUTE.

BA-DUMP

BA-DUMP BA-DUMP

BUT...

I DON'T KNOW!!!

That's what I'd like to know, too!

SHINODA MASAKO@DRB48-SAN ASKS: "WHY IS JUNKER-SAN A VIRGIN?"

SO?! SO WHAT?!

You're so mean!

SHOCK

Y-YOU'RE A YOKAI, SO...

Relevant in Me

Give us your questions!
We'd love to hear your questions for the characters! Please follow Rokka's account on Twitter (@panyanyaruru) to ask questions and begin your reply with [Question]! Rokka and the other characters in *Yokai Girls* will respond!

Yokai Field Guide!

Introducing the yokai Yatsuki has encountered in Yokai Girls-style!

Kappas possessing humans is a big part of the folklore of western Japan. Typically, it's said that a kappa will possess a young woman, making her go around saying obscene things, hit on men, and become lascivious. In Kusu district, Ooita prefecture, it was believed that virgin women were most easily targeted, and that possession would cause them to become seriously ill and die. In order to free a woman from possession by a kappa, she had to be tied up with straw rope and exorcised. However, if in the process, the straw rope were to get wet, the spirits of water would restore the kappa's power and it would tear the rope to shreds.

First Appearance: Chapter 24

河童憑き

KAPPA POSSESSION

KAPPA-TSUKI

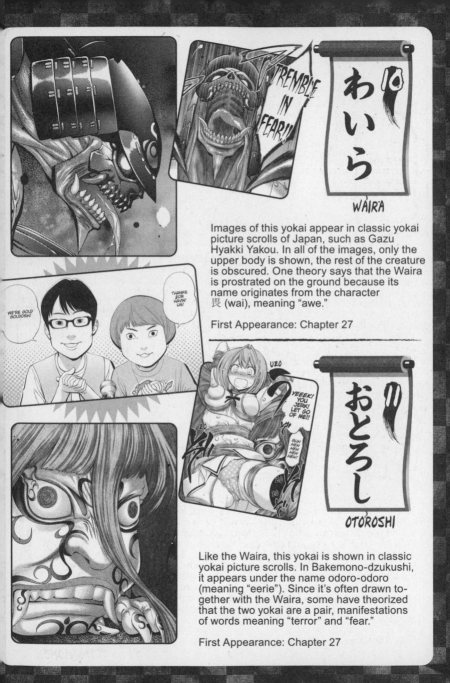

わいら

WAIRA

Images of this yokai appear in classic yokai picture scrolls of Japan, such as Gazu Hyakki Yakou. In all of the images, only the upper body is shown, the rest of the creature is obscured. One theory says that the Waira is prostrated on the ground because its name originates from the character 畏 (wai), meaning "awe."

First Appearance: Chapter 27

おとろし

OTOROSHI

Like the Waira, this yokai is shown in classic yokai picture scrolls. In Bakemono-dzukushi, it appears under the name odoro-odoro (meaning "eerie"). Since it's often drawn together with the Waira, some have theorized that the two yokai are a pair, manifestations of words meaning "terror" and "fear."

First Appearance: Chapter 27

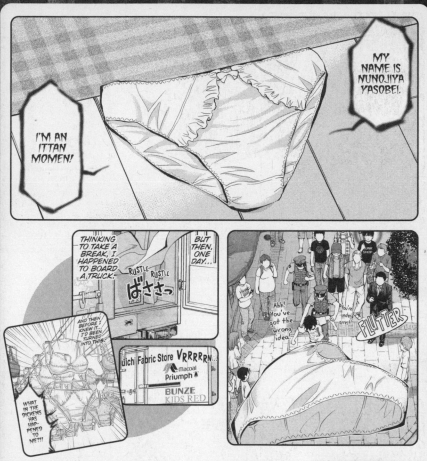

Tales of this yokai have been told in Takayama, Kimotsuki district, in Kagoshima. They say that cloth measuring one-tenth hectare long (10.6m long, 30cm wide) will flutter through the sky, and then attack people. It wraps around the head, suffocating its victim to death, then envelops its victim to fly away, carrying the body into the sky. The ittan momen is said to appear at dusk. One theory says that parents busy with farm work and unable to watch their children at this time of day used stories of the ittan momen to warn their children to return home quickly.

First Appearance: Chapter 28

一反木綿

12

(ONE-TENTH HECT-ARE COTTON)

ITTAN MOMEN

Don Quijote

Akihabara
UDX

Animate

Tora no Ana
Flagship
Akihabara
Shops

Akihabara
Dai Building

Yodobashi Camera
Yuurindou

JR Akihabara Station

Radio Kaikan

K-Books

SEVEN SEAS' GHOST SHIP PRESENTS

YOKAI GIRLS

story and art by **KAZUKI FUNATSU**

VOL.**3**

TRANSLATION
Jennifer Ward

ADAPTATION
Bambi Eloriaga-Amago

LETTERING AND LAYOUT
Phil Christie

COVER DESIGN
Nicky Lim

PROOFREADER
Janet Houck
Stephanie Cohen

EDITOR
J.P. Sullivan
Shannon Fay

PRODUCTION ASSISTANT
CK Russell

PRODUCTION MANAGER
Lissa Pattillo

EDITOR-IN-CHIEF
Adam Arnold

PUBLISHER
Jason DeAngelis

YOKAI SHOJO-MONSTER GIRL VOL. 3
© 2014 Kazuki Funatsu
All rights reserved.
First published in 2014 by SHUEISHA Inc. Tokyo.
English translation rights arranged by SHUEISHA Inc.
through TOHAN CORPORATION, Tokyo.

No portion of this book may be reproduced or transmitted in any form without
written permission from the copyright holders. This is a work of fiction. Names,
characters, places, and incidents are the products of the author's imagination
or are used fictitiously. Any resemblance to actual events, locales, or persons,
living or dead, is entirely coincidental.

Seven Seas, Ghost Ship, and their accompanying logos are trademarks of
Seven Seas Entertainment, LLC. All rights reserved.

ISBN: 978-1-947804-05-0

Printed in Canada

First Printing: May 2018

10 9 8 7 6 5 4 3 2 1

FOLLOW US ONLINE: *www.ghostshipmanga.com*

READING DIRECTIONS

This book reads from *right to left*, Japanese style.
If this is your first time reading manga, you start
reading from the top right panel on each page and
[...] from there. If you get lost, just follow the
[...] diagram here. It may seem backwards at
[...]'ll get the hang of it! Have fun!!

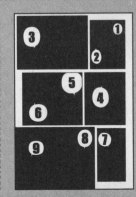